Tell Don't Show
How to successfully break the RULES of FICTION

by
Nicole J. Persun
Susan Wingate
Terry Persun

For our students and fellow authors.

Table of Contents

Welcome Rulebreakers!

What a wonderful group of writers we are, we who are interested in how to break writing rules. And rightfully so. We wouldn't want to read a book where the writer was trying so hard to fit into some box of limitations that they weren't happy during the process of writing. The book wouldn't flow. The author would be forcing narrative. Most likely dialogue and plot would sound as though it had been pulled from an outline instead of life or passion or creativity.

Are we saying you have to break the rules to be happy with your writing? To be an accomplished writer? Yes, we are. If you're a real writer, a real artist, you want to knock all the walls down, throw caution to the wind, get people to think about the world or themselves in a new and different way—expand the envelope. You want to make a statement, even if you consider your books and stories as entertainment. And the best way to do this is to break some rules, rules you often hear other experts spouting off. Still, like anything else, knowing the rules and why they exist in the first place, is a good place to start.

We're amazed when we attend writers' conferences and notice that some instructors begin by talking about the rules of writing as though breaking them would lead to instant rejection. Those rules include: avoid adverbs, don't use too much passive voice, start with action, show don't tell—you get the idea. But no writer has stuck to all of the rules we've heard taught. And you won't either. The question isn't whether or not you're breaking the rules, it's whether or not you know what the rules are, why they're in place, and then how to break them well and on purpose.

This little book is going to look at a lot of different rules. First, we'll tell you what the rule is; second, we'll explain why we believe the rule was originally started (you know, what makes doing these things so damned irritating to some editors and/or readers); and third, we'll proceed to explain how to break the rule with some semblance of success, including examples from bestselling and critically acclaimed authors.

We do want to alert you to the fact that not everyone agrees on what works and what doesn't. And, you must know that every nonfiction book is merely the opinion of its author(s). We're no different. So, you're going to get our opinion here. If you don't always agree with us, that's okay. Go to your bookshelf and find your own examples, ones you can sink your teeth into.

By the end of this book you will have a handle on how you can break the rules of fiction consciously, how rule-breaking can help the flow of your work, and why writers break rules at all.

Thank you and enjoy,

Nicole Persun, Terry Persun, and Susan Wingate

Rule 1: Start With Action
Bullets flew and windows shattered, leaving nothing alive in the room.

How many times have you heard something along these lines spoken by some pro at a writers' conference?

- "You must start with action, otherwise the reader won't get hooked!"
- "If something doesn't happen on the first page, why would a reader keep reading?"
- "Drop the reader right into the middle of the action!"

The Start-with-Action rule is in place, we're sure, because many manuscripts tend to begin by dumping a lot of information on the first page. Information–dumping reads like textbook copy and *explains* who the character is or what the problem is or something like the fact that the room is 12-feet-square with about 8-foot high walls.

One of our pet peeves is when first sentence starts out with someone's full given name with additional physical details immediately after. For example, "Harold Wilbur Collingswood stood a good six feet ten, but weighed less than 200 pounds. His lean body was acquired through vigorous training…" Unless this has something very significant to do with the next few sentences, it's not going to get anyone to keep reading.

And then there are books where in the first few chapters all you get are introductions to different characters, one by boring one. Or the book opens with a flowery scene of the hillside and creek that goes on and on, page after page, and you have no idea how it relates to the story at all. Or worse, the book starts with some abstract emotional verbiage that's supposed to drag you into the sorrow and pain of the main character—before you even know the character well enough to care.

The real point to this rule is to *hook the reader*. But there are many ways to hook the reader, and starting with action is only one of them.

We all can tell when an author is trying too hard, or more worried that we'll not understand something and therefore provides way too much background detail. Renni Brown talks about this error in her book, *Self-editing for Fiction Authors* (written with Dave King). She tells us how we should "resist the urge to explain" and gives us a great tool—the acronym RUE to drive home her point.

When the reader doesn't have a clue who the main character is, or hasn't had the chance to get to know them, no methodical or abrupt beginning is going to matter to that reader in the long run. Hooking the reader is about piquing their interest but, more importantly, building their emotional investment in the character. Reveal information on why your main character carries all the risk and reward of your novel. Entice the reader with a glimpse into your character's psyche: their problems, their desires, their internal world.

Knowing who your reader is helps too. There are readers who prefer a slow beginning, yet it can be equally preferable to start a book with bullets or fists flying. Understanding the tropes of your genre will help narrow down the ideal beginning for your book. Read the first page or two of the top ten books in your genre and you'll get an idea what those readers expect from you.

Let's look at *Into the Looking Glass* by John Ringo. *Into the Looking Glass* is a military sci-fi novel. He starts with action.

> The explosion, later categorized as in the near equivalent of 60 kilotons of TNT and centered on the University of Central Florida, occurred at 9:28 A.M. on a Saturday in early March, a calm spring day in Orlando when the sky was clear and the air was cool and, for Florida, reasonably dry. It occurred entirely without warning and while it originated at the university the effects were felt far outside its grounds.

The first two words tell you there is an explosion. This opens the door for the reader to ask questions: Why is this happening? What's going to happen next? Who's behind it? etc. Getting the reader to ask questions is all part of piquing their interest. You want the reader to begin asking questions so they will be compelled to read on in order to find the answers. You want your reader to become invested — riveted, even — as soon as possible, so that they will continue to turn pages.

Here's a second example of a novel that starts out with action, although a different kind of action. This is from *Scar Lover* by Harry Crews, a mainstream love story.

> Peter Butcher had not meant to speak to her. And he probably would not have if she had not stared at him so directly as she stepped out of the shade of the oak tree in front of her house to stand in the sun on the sidewalk. The only place he had seen her before was in the yard, close to the trunk of the tree, dim as a ghost in the deep shade. But this morning he had to pass within a foot or two of her because she had come out to stand on the sidewalk.

Something is going on here. We can feel the tension. However, the action is subtle. She stares at him. She steps out of the shade and stands near the sidewalk. He must come close to her. For some this might appear just a bit too creepy, but no matter what you're thinking about the story at this time, it's got you hooked, and not much has really gone on. It's the promise of something more to come that draws you into the story. Crews gets the reader asking, "What happens once Peter speaks to her?"

Now, let's look at an example of how suspense, interest, and tension can be built without any action at all. The next excerpt if from C. C. Humphreys' novel *Vlad: The Last Confession*, a historical novel about the real Vlad Dracula. Humphreys is a master at drawing the reader in with tension.

> All was still in the forest. The last snowflakes of the sudden storm had just fallen. Everything paused.
> In the crook of a copper beech sat a man. His arms were crossed, gloved hands folded into his lap, the

right beneath to support the weight of the goshawk
on his left. They had been there for a long time, as
long as the blizzard lasted. Man and bird—part of
the stillness, part of the silence. Both had their eyes
closed. Neither were asleep.

Tension, in this beginning, is built by showing us the calm *after* the
storm, which gives a foreshadowing of the present calm before the
present storm. We're immediately interested in what's going on. Who
is this man? What's he waiting for? How does the goshawk play into
the story? Although this page does not start with action, we want to
continue due to the suggestion of movement later on. What happens
when the man and the bird break their pause and are no longer still?

And another somewhat slow beginning comes from thriller novel,
The Last Detective by Robert Crais. It's not until the last sentence of
the first paragraph that we get sucked into the story, even though we
have been led masterfully right into it.

The cold Alaskan water pulled at the fishing boats
that lined the dock, the boats straining against their
moorings to run free with the tide. The water here
in the small harbor at Angoon, a fishing village on
the western shore of Admiralty Island off southeast
Alaska, was steel-black beneath the clouds and
dimpled by rain, but was clear even with that, a
window beneath the weathered pilings to a world of
sunburst starfish as wide as garbage cans, jellyfish
the size of basketballs, and barnacles as heavy as a
longshoreman's fist. Alaska was like that, so vigorous
with life that it could fill a man and lift him and maybe
even bring him back from the dead.

Many books begin with an image that brings about all sorts of
questions. That's really the idea. As mentioned earlier, pure emotional
content doesn't work because it becomes abstract and difficult to
define pretty quickly. An image—whether an explosion or a man
sitting in a tree, whether a woman stepping out from the shadows or
the boats docked at a harbor—helps to draw the reader into the story

on their own terms.

Sometimes a beautiful scene of flowering gardens will end up foreshadowing something sinister to the reader, or it will even foreshadow someone's love interest. Sometimes similar scenes just like this one will go nowhere and cause a reader to put the book down. The language used, the turn of the phrase, can be the difference between the reader giving up on the first page, or allowing themselves to be led down the long path to the end of the novel.

So, hooking a reader at the beginning of your novel is not always about starting with a clichéd version of action. It's about tugging at the readers' interests—whether with magical writing, sinister foreshadowing, or a character's longing.

The takeaway for this section is to learn how to draw your reader into your story. It's something you can study by reading other books in the genre you're writing, but also by reading books in genres outside your interests.

Play around with your beginnings. Practice with your own writing.

One time practice your beginning using movement and motion. The next time, practice using an arresting image.

Whether you want to hook the reader through action or tension is up to you, your genre, your reader, and what you think is best for *your* book. It's just important for you to know that you won't be doomed if your book doesn't start with a car chase or a murder.

One last thought to consider about hooking your reader... In the John Ringo and Robert Crais excerpts there are no mentions of specific characters. This would alert me right away that these stories are plot-driven novels. Right off the bat, we become invested in the what's going on in the story (the plot), not the people.

These writers do this intentionally. Equally, some readers enjoy a fast-paced plot that the right books deliver from the start.

Vlad, and *Star Lover*, on the other hand, are more character-driven novels where the author highlights character first.

Remember, however, that plot-driven and character-driven novels don't always start out this way. But for our examples, we contrast the genres this way because they fit well for purposes of explaining "the novel hook."

Rule 2: Show Don't Tell

The velvet curtain changed from royal to navy under the lekos. The body lay still, blood oozing out its life onto the stage.

We could say that all stories are told, and it would be true. Still, what the rule Show Don't Tell refers to, more than anything else, is the use of language.

Abstract, vague, ambiguous language tells you something, but doesn't have the same impact as image-driven adjectives or action verbs.

For example, "He came into the office angry," is hardly as satisfying to read as, "He clomped into the office, pounding one fist into the palm of his other, and squinting his eyes before bursting out with his complaint." In the second example, the character is angry through action. You don't need to be told.

This rule is in place simply because of all those flat, uninteresting descriptions, such as, "Jed *looked* nervous," or "the young hairstylist *was* pretty."

So, what's Jed doing that makes you think that? How does he portray nervousness? Is he shaking? Glancing around the room? Does he appear pale or queasy?

And show me how the hairstylist is pretty. Is her skin smooth as soapstone? Are her eyes the color of a teal lake? Does her shape appear like that of a runway model's shape?

Depending on the viewpoint in your story, showing details through the *lens* of your character can also be revealing to his or her personality and the way in which he or she interacts with the world. For instance, perhaps your viewpoint character only *thinks* Jed looks nervous, because your viewpoint character shakes just like that when she's nervous (when in reality, she might learn later on, Jed is shaking for another reason, perhaps with anger). The same goes for the hairstylist. If your viewpoint character thinks the hairstylist is pretty due to her long blonde hair, that might say something about your viewpoint character's taste in women.

When description is important to the story line readers don't want to be told. They want to be shown, to see, touch, hear, smell, and taste that description for themselves because when we see, touch, hear, smell, and taste something for ourselves, we have sensory responders to the thing we are seeing, touching, hearing, smelling, and tasting. Readers want to live the experience just as much as we, the author, want to write it.

So, let's discuss briefly how to get three levels of information across to the reader.

> • Level one is the *flat abstraction*: "Jed looked nervous." This level almost always includes an abstract word like angry, love, hate, shock. We all know what angry looks like in general, but we don't know what it looks like when it's attached to Jed. And we're not being shown, either.
> • Level two is *showing through description.* "Sweat beaded along Jed's upper lip as though it were hot in the room. His shirt tail hung out, forgotten or left that way because something else was suddenly more important."
> • Level three is *showing through action.* "Jed shifted from foot to foot as though dancing, his hands never stopped shaking, and he couldn't keep his eyes on me the whole time he was there."

The problem with this rule is how too many writers go overboard with showing. They describe every movement. They show the trees bending and the roadway edges. They show what the character is wearing, what the weather is like, what type of car the character gets into, a list of all the stores on the block... At that point, you might was well watch a movie. The book becomes so rife with showing that the reader loses track of the story and therefore loses track of *what's important.* Too much showing obscures important details, often to the point of boredom.

So, the real point of Show Don't Tell is to make your *most important* images strong. Don't include detail just for the sake of detail and because you're trying to show and not tell. That's overdoing the point of this rule.

Instead, include detail when it's *necessary* —when without the detail, the story is weaker.

Our personal guideline (which we believe is most important here) is this: To ask, does the description reveal something about the character? Does it move the story forward? If showing through description or action does *not* add to these items, then just utilize telling in your narrative or dialogue.

Furthermore, if we've been reading and are halfway through a novel and one of the characters is always slamming things around and yelling, then for goodness sake don't describe this behavior every time.

It's okay to say, *He burst through one door after another, angrier each time he crashed through.*

Here's a good example of telling that works. It's from *Homer and Langley* by E. L. Doctorow:

> Despite the assurances of his letter, my brother
> returned as a different man. His voice was a kind of
> gargle and he kept coughing and clearing his throat.
> He had been a clear tenor when he left, and would
> sing the old arias as I played them. Not now.

In this passage, the main character, Homer, *tells* us first about his brother. Even though we don't see his brother coughing, and although we don't hear his gargled voice, the main character *tells* us how his brother sounds. What happens is we learn to know our characters fairly well from this passage, and our hearts go out to them.

At the beginning of the novel, Doctorow shows us as Homer loses his eyesight.

> What I did this particular winter was to stand back
> from the lake in Central Park where they did all their
> ice skating and see what I could see and couldn't see

as a day-by-day thing. The houses over Central Park West went first, they got darker as if dissolving into the dark sky until I couldn't make them out, and then the trees began to lose their shape, and then finally, this was toward the end of the season, maybe it was late February of that very cold winter, and all I could see were these phantom shapes of the ice skaters floating past me on a field of ice, and then a white ice, that last light, went gray and then altogether black, and then all my sight was gone though I could hear clearly the scoot scut of the blades on the ice...

It's important to notice in these two examples that Doctorow uses showing *and* telling. A skilled writer knows when telling is better for the story, and vice versa.

The takeaway for the Show Don't Tell rule is to show only when what you're describing is most important to character development, story progress, or plot details that will be used later. Otherwise, it's okay to tell the reader a few things to set the scene. After all, you don't want to bog your reader down with long, drawn out passages that do nothing more than show.

Rule 3: Don't Use Adverbs
The natives were frighteningly savage.

This is an *unbelievably* silly rule! Just kidding. But, honestly, we need to make a point of this rule, too.

A lot of instructors that we've had the pleasure of working with, and a lot of the books we've read on how to write, suggest that using *ly* adverbs (and adjectives, for that matter) make writers look lazy.

This is a subset rule of showing. Do you see that? Instead of *showing* a character jogging with little coordination down the road using action verbs, we shorten the sentence by saying that the character jogged *awkwardly*. When we use adverbs such as this, the reader is never shown what *awkwardly* really means, and instead is left to imagine what the author intends the word *awkwardly* to look like.

Another reason for this rule is that many writers use adverbs in a redundant manner. An example of redundant use in adverbs is when a character, "shouts *loudly*," where the word *shouts* would have sufficed. In this instance, the adverb is rendered completely unnecessary due to the verbs' ability to hold its own. Other situations might include someone who *quickly* raced out of the room, or someone whose hand shook *nervously*.

People in the know say adverbs disrupt the flow, the musicality, of a scene. Tacking an adverb onto the end of a dialogue tag is one such use. It makes the sentence awkward. Plus, "...she said quietly" can pull you out of a scene where "...she whispered" has the opposite affect.

The real point to this rule, of course, is *don't be lazy*. Always try to come up with the right word versus tacking on an adverb for emphasis. Especially if you're writing an action scene, don't revert to using adverbs to help explain everything. Your character doesn't want to load his gun quickly, anxiously start shooting, and frighteningly hide behind the table. Adverbs used this way tend to weigh down action. Below we compare the actual sentences.

With Adverbs:

He loaded his gun quickly, anxiously started shooting, and hid frighteningly behind the table.

Without Adverbs:

He loaded his gun, started shooting, and hid behind the table.

As you can see, the action scene written without adverbs is a faster, more action-packed sentence. That's exactly what we hope for in writing action scenes.

Now, consider this:

Lily Tuck, a literary writer and one of our favorites, uses adverbs often, but with great literary effect. Here's an example from her novel, *I Married You for Happiness*:

> Gently, with her index finger, she turns the gold
> band on his ring finger round and round.

See how the adverb *gently*, placed at the very beginning, carries the action throughout the rest of the sentence? Normally, one would write: She turns the ring on his finger round and round, gently. Or: She gently turns the ring on his ring finger, round and round. Or, without the adverb altogether: With her index finger, she turns the gold band on his ring finger round and round. Yet, Tuck puts her adverb, *gently*, right up front so that it says more than just how she turned the gold band, but says something about their relationship and how she feels about the person's on whose finger she is turning the ring. And she does it all at once with a single adverb. It might appear to make only a slight distinction, but it's an important one. Tuck has chosen that word and its placement for greatest effect.

A line from Philip Roth's award-winning short story, *Goodbye Columbus*, brings up another interesting point about adverbs. Here's the sentence:

> I walked rather bouncingly up the lawn, past the
> huge weeping willow, towards the waiting Patimkins,
> wishing all the while that I'd had my car washed.

The adverb we're considering here is *bouncingly*. Why does it work? First of all, it's written in the first person point of view. One could argue that, because the character is narrating, he isn't going to explain, in detail, what his bouncy walk looks like. He can't see himself in order to describe it, so he states what he does know, which is the feeling of the bounce.

Still, another thing to note with this image is the fact that his walk isn't what we want to focus on in this scene. Later in the sentence (and in the story), the reader understands that it's the unwashed car and his relaxed nature that the author is trying to get across. The scene is all about characterization. The scene as a whole is what we want to understand, not the specific showing of his walk. One could argue that describing his walk with more detail in order to cut the adverb wouldn't hurt the scene, but by keeping the line concise, we can continue forward through the scene to his interactions with the family, which is where the story is going. And, unless this character has some neurological disease that is important to the story and important to describing his appearance and how he walks (think *My Left Foot* by Christy Brown), then we simply need to get through this scene and onto the telling of the story as the story relates to this very important first scene—one drenched in character development for the reader.

Another thought about this particular adverb, *bouncingly*. It's also an active word (and bounces off the tongue!). To write, he *bouncingly* walked up the lawn, is possibly better than, "I walked up the lawn" or worse, "I went up the lawn." *Bouncingly* offers movement, a sense of mood and heaps of characterization.

The takeaway for this rule is to use your words. All of them. Selectively and intentionally. When you come across an adverb in your work, ask yourself, "Was this adverb intended, was it planned, deliberate?" and "Would I be willing to stand up for this adverb is an editor wanted me to cut it?" and "Is this scene better with the adverb than without?" If the scene would be better if you cut it, then cut it!

But if the adverb has an intended purpose and adds to the scene, then leave it!

Also, try moving your adverbs around in your sentences to see where they are most effective. Do you want to shock your reader with the adverb at the end of the sentence, or lead the reader through how to read the sentence by placing the adverb at the beginning? We often recommend that novelists study poetry, because poetry helps in learning to refine your writing and your use of words with more care. Poetry also helps you understand tempo and musicality in your sentences.

As an added bonus, here are a few examples of how adverbs (and not just the ly adverbs we often demonize!) might be used:

- Emphasizers (or amplifiers): I *really* don't believe him. He *literally* wrecked his mother's car. She *simply* ignored me. They're going to be late, *for sure*. I *always* see him at work. The teacher *completely* rejected the proposal. I *absolutely* refuse to attend any more faculty meetings. They *heartily* endorsed the new restaurant. I *so* wanted to go with them. We know this city *well*. He *never* got sick.

- Downtoners: I *kind of* like this college. Joe *sort of* felt betrayed by his sister. His mother *mildly* disapproved of his actions. We can improve on this *to some extent*. The boss *almost* quit after that. The school was *all but* ruined by the storm.

Adverbs are parts of speech, after all, and since they exist in our language, we might as well use them in our writing. But when you do, use them conscientiously and your work will read *swimmingly* better because of it.

Rule 4: Avoid Passive Voice

She is by far the most passive woman. I was like her once. But I changed.

Before we get started with this chapter, we'd like to quote Steven Pinker from his book *The Sense of Style: the Thinking Person's Guide to Writing in the 21st Century!*.

> Linguistic research has shown that the passive construction has a number of indispensable functions because of the way it engages a reader's attention and memory.

Pinker's quote says a lot about passive voice that you won't hear in writing classes, and must be considered whenever you're writing your novel. Having begun this chapter thusly, we'd like to say that many people don't even know the difference between an active and a passive voice. This is where we will start.

In normal sentences, a subject performs an action. For example: Robert threw the ball. *Robert* is the subject and *threw* is the action. In a passive sentence, the subject is acted upon rather than performing the action: The ball *was thrown* by Robert. Or, Robert *was throwing* the ball.

The reason this rule exists is because passive voice sentences are often longer, more awkward, and sometimes more vague than active voice. People use passive voice without even realizing it. Overusing passive voice can be problematic regardless of the fact that it can engage a reader's attention and memory. Used too often, passive voice creates boring writing where no one ever takes action.

The real point has as much to do about being clear and concise as it has about creating actions for our readers to follow. So, a lot of instructors who are touting this rule are merely trying to get writers to use active verbs whenever possible, and to focus on the subject of the sentence and the action taking place.

All of this can be accomplished simply by being aware of your sentence structure. What are you trying to emphasize? Do you want to emphasize what Robert is doing, or do you want to emphasize what's happening to the ball? Are Robert's parents watching him throw the ball? Or is his older sister, the owner of the ball, more concerned with the ball than with Robert. (For instance: The ball that hit her in the head was thrown by Robert.) All this depends upon the point of view you wish to take and what you want your readers to take away from the sentence and scene.

For highly action-packed books, we often suggest that a passive sentence placed here and there will keep the reader from feeling beaten up or getting exhausted from reading only action sentences. If your verbs are always active, the book begins to sound like a machine gun. If the writer simply changes the verb (even though similar activities are going on), your work can read like some kind of strange power dance.

But, writing intermittent passive sentences can help your prose to read smoother by slowing things down, by changing phrasing and adding pace, and by giving your prose more variety.

The next example of passive voice is from a novel that is highly active called *Into the Looking Glass* by John Ringo. We mentioned earlier that this book has been written in the genre called military science fiction. Ringo's story has a lot of going on throughout the book. However, he's placed a passive break within all the active sentences:

> The burst of radiation that had come from the gate
> had, fortunately, been blocked by the hill.

Written actively, this sentence might read: The hill blocked the burst of radiation coming from the gate.

We can't say what John was thinking when he wrote this sentence, but it could have been that he recognized that the reader might need a rest. Maybe he, himself, was getting tired of all the action—of one thing happening after the other, over and again. So, he gave it a break.

It could also be that Ringo wanted the reader to focus on the burst of radiation. Maybe he purposely placed that part of the sentence first so that the reader would *feel* the burst of radiation, to give them a physical sensation.

If so, this would instantly create concern in the reader—"Oh no! A burst of radiation!"—before telling the reader that the radiation was *blocked* by the hill. Because, remember, we've been reading in a trot all the way up to the instance of radiation bursting!

Once the reader knows that the radiation was *blocked*, their initial excitement or worry might turn to relief. Manipulating a reader's emotions is what great writing is all about.

In Ringo's example, we see that sentence structure has many purposes. As a writer, you've got to use your reasons wisely and to their greatest effect. Sometimes using the passive voice allows the writer to manipulate the reader in just the right way to keep them eager to read further.

Here's the takeaway on when it's okay to use passive voice: as it is with other rules, *it depends*. Even if you love those short, direct sentences because they help you write clearly, you might find you've written a scene where the writing feels choppy or far too active. Hammering your reader over the head isn't what good writing is about. You don't want to exhaust your reader.

Remember, in some cases, you might decide to slow all of the action. And, in other cases, you might want to set your reader up so that they feel relief, or interest or excitement. Your reason might also be that you want to place some kind of important information up front, and that important information is best serviced in a passive sentence. If for no other reason at all but to alter your pacing, passive voice has a lot to offer.

So, it's best to add a little passive voice to the mix while writing your next novel. Keep in mind that you'll want to know that you're including it purposefully and understand why you chose a passive passage over an active one. And if an early reader or editor complains that you're using passive voice, examine that section for lack of clarity or a sagging pace. If neither is the case, you might want to remind them that a little passive voice can be a good thing, a way to break up your prose with some variety.

It may be that passive voice is used so precisely that it creates an ebb and flow to the work, like an ocean tide that first crashes against the shore, then recedes quietly back into the sea, only to gain energy for the next crash.

Rule 5: Don't Use Fragmented Sentences

An empty street. And the hollow sound, oh, the sound.

What? Inconceivable! This is one of our favorite rules to break. Totally.

The rule itself started way back when we were kids and were first taught the components of a simple sentence.

A sentence had to have: a subject, a verb, and a predicate (something the subject acted upon). For instance: Tom hit the ball. Jane wadded the paper. Spot chewed the bone.

A simple sentence is easy to understand. Notice how these *simple* sentences employ the use of action.

Everything with simple sentence structure is laid out in an orderly fashion. It's logical. That's the reason we have this rule in the first place.

The rule to not fragment sentences was created to maintain clarity. You can't argue with a simple sentence. You won't get confused or wonder what's happening. Everything is laid out in sequential sentence order—subject, verb, predicate. You know who (subject) is acting. You know what they did (verb). And you know what they did it to (predicate). If you have any missing parts, suddenly the sentence is not as clear anymore. Your reader will stop dead in her tracks.

Besides, how can a reader go on if they don't know what just happened? (Insert sarcastic groan here. Let's please give our readers credit. They, after all, um, *read!*) And what happens if an author writes several fragments in a row? Heavens! The world is going to stop! Certainly, right? Won't this compound the reader's confusion, thusly, making the reader put down your book?

Pfft! Readers are intelligent human beings who can see that fragments are placed on purpose.

So, how can we break this rule without causing the reader undue confusion?

First, let's understand that if a fragment is deleted it will invariably be almost impossible to know what's going on. If deleting the fragment does not cause confusion, then the critics of fragments would be correct in their rule-setting. But, here's the truth: fragments are written within a larger context. And, this is where the rule becomes something less than perfect.

Dragged out of context, the following fragment from James Salter's *Light Years* has the reader perplexed:

Not a ship, not a dinghy, not one cry of white.

What does this fragmented sentence mean? Out of context, we don't know. It might be beautiful scene-setting, but who cares? And, because of the nouns, you might be able to create a general idea of what's going on, or *not*.

What we love about this quote is that the fragment appears on the first page of the story. In fact, it's the second sentence (or fragmented sentence).

Here's Salter's first sentence:

We dash the black river, its flats smooth as stone.

With this sentence, the reader begins to see a picture, which allows the fragment to fill in the gaps, as it were. So, now we have:

We dash the black river, its flats smooth as stone.
Not a ship, not a dinghy, not one cry of white.

Then, the paragraph goes on after these first two with similarly image-driven sentences. Let's look at how Salter's fragmented sentence plays into the whole of his work:

We dash the black river, its flats smooth as stone. Not a ship, not a dinghy, not one cry of white. The water lies broken, cracked from the wind. This great estuary is wide, endless. The river is brackish, blue with the cold.

For our ears, the fragment adds flavor to the writing. The style is simple, the sentence structure often repeated, except for that second sentence—a poetic one—which somehow offers a foreshadowing, might we suggest, of there being something missing.

Perhaps Mr. Salter didn't plan that, maybe it was by accident. But perhaps he did. Either way, it works.

In Terry Persun's novel *The Witness Tree*, he borrowed Salter's idea to use a fragment in this way, for this purpose.

In the clear, pink morning, at dawn.

As did Salter, Terry used his fragment in his second sentence on the first page. Terry's first sentence is:

I remember clear back to the first day they began to move the trucks and other heavy equipment in.

It's not like a reader wouldn't know something important about the setting just by this fragment. It's a standalone image. But with the first sentence, the reader is taken to a precise place and time where (and when) heavy equipment is being brought in.

Again, after his fragment, Terry uses a few simple sentences, aimed at grounding the reader and getting them back into the story so that any slightest confusion will now be rooted in simplicity.

Here are those first sentences all together:

I remember clear back to the first day they began to move the trucks and other heavy equipment in. In the clear, pink morning, at dawn. It was early spring. All the animals became alarmed.

From here, Terry writes a long, complex sentence. Then he goes back to short simple sentences. This back and forth takes the reader on a ride not only of pacing, but of focus from large to small, the wider view and the detail. One other thing the fragment does is foreshadow the beautiful confusion that the main character goes through in this novel.

So, how many fragments can an author use before the reader throws the book across the room? That, of course, depends on what you're writing about, how the fragments proceed from one to the next, and of the reader's ability to follow along. This is a flexible rule, like all writing rules.

We suggest that you read passages aloud, or tape them and then play them back. If you can follow along, then hopefully your reader will be able to as well.

A final note.

Although Terry's book was published by a small, independent publisher, *Implosion Press*, it was also republished and distributed by another small press, *Russell Dean and Company*. When the publisher at *Russell Dean and Company* first read *The Witness Tree*, he said he almost rejected the book after the first page because of the fragment. But he read on and loved the book so much that he signed Terry's book for second printing rights.

After that, the novel was picked up by a third small press, *Booktrope Editions*. So, even with a fragment on the first page, editors—who are often looking for something wrong just so they can reject a book—passed through the fragment without much of a hitch. This is not to say that a different editor might be so inclined. But if done well, and if the author grounds the reader in a few simple sentences afterward, the chances are that your fragment will pass the test and be accepted too.

Let's look at another example, one in which the scene *relies* on the fragments to convey character and emotion within a scene. This one is from Judith Guest's *Ordinary People* (an example also used in the wonderful book by Priscilla Long, *The Writer's Portable Mentor*). In this scene, two parents just learned that their son drowned.

> They had neither of them cried that night on the dock. Too awesome, too catastrophic for tears. That murderous, lead-colored moon. The sky, wispy with cloud-strings. The black water all around them, indistinguishable from the black sky. The people

who didn't know who they were, only that something
terrible had happened.

It's a powerful paragraph, with five fragments in a row. The reader is transported into a moment of trauma, where the parents feel shattered, *fragmented*, themselves. They can't form coherent thoughts, so what they notice are images broken up. The moon. The sky. The other people standing around, not knowing exactly what had happened, only that it was terrible.

In this case, the writing not only is filled with beautiful fragmented images, one after another, it also mirrors the characters and their emotions. Similarly, an author might use fragments to convey excitement, or concern, or any number of other emotions, depending on what images are used as focal points.

The takeaway, as for most of these rules, is to write with intention. Why use a fragment here? What does it add to the scene? Writing, after all, is an art, and that rule we learned as kids about sentences versus sentence fragments is only the baseline for what an author can do with his or her words, characters, and storyline.

Rule 6: Refrain From Word Repetition
Do not ever, ever, ever repeat words!

This is a favorite rule of many editors—all three authors of this book have experienced a reader or editor who was fixated on this rule above all else. Often, if an editor notices the second usage of a word in the same paragraph or on the same page, he'll make a note that you're using the same word too often. He might even suggest other words to use. For instance, if you used the words *technique, house,* or *rhythm* more than once, that editor might suggest you use *method* for technique, or *residence* for house, *cadence* for rhythm. We've all read passages where an author uses similar words rather than the same word. It's so obvious that doing so the editor has created another distraction for the passage—the distraction of *avoidance.*

However, there are those authors who will take this rule to heart. These authors are often so concerned about repeating words that they keep a Thesaurus open on their desktop while writing. This act, in itself, is enough to make your writing choppy.

If an author is writing about a neighborhood where he grew up, for example, and he uses the word *house* one time, *home* another, *residence* another, *habitat* another, *abode* another, and *domicile* yet another, the text is going to sound weird and be confusing.

With no repetition you have to ask: Is a house a home? Is an abode a domicile? Or is it a *habitat*? Of course they are.

But, this kind of word switching stands out and you don't want specific words to stand out, you want your story to.

So, what do we do, then, to avoid redundancy and not sound redundant? (Ha!) Well, it might be worth considering the use of only two similar words and alternating them. Using the words *house* and *home* repeatedly might not be enough to break up the repetition, but it wouldn't introduce additional problems with sound, tempo, and meaning if you introduced more words like *abode* and *habitat*.

The basic rule is: refrain from using the same word over and over to the point the reader will notice, and be taken out of your story. It makes sense too in the broader sense but, like every other rule, it might not make sense for a particular passage.

The underlying issue here, a belief among editors, perhaps, is that if you use the same word repeatedly you're doing so because you have a limited vocabulary, and possibly indicates a limited education. Or, simply, you're a lazy writer and you aren't taking time to find a *better* word, one that's more accurate and fits the passage properly. And, honestly, any of these perceptions could be true. That's why the rule is in place to begin with. Our suggestion is to avoid being seen as a lazy writer. Make sure that you're language—every single word—shows conscious choice and not just the first word that pops up.

We believe the real point of the rule is to help the author look more intelligently at word choice than they might actually do (of course, do this when you're editing your manuscript, not while writing the first draft, otherwise you'll get hung up on word choice and never finish getting the story down!). Don't we, after all, want our writing to be the best that it can be?

Because of this perception—that you'd have to be either lazy or stupid to repeat words in your story—breaking this rule is something that we particularly enjoy.

When breaking this rule consciously, purposefully, repetition can add depth and beauty to your writing and a sense of poetry, tempo and mood. In *Wilderness* by Robert Penn Warren, one of our favorite passages in this story is one that rolls from repeated word to repeated word:

> Then, out of the timelessness of the road, white oxen topped the rise, the wagon coming into sight now. The oxen came on, white in the white road, white dust rising sleepily about their knees, dust stirred...

Notice how Mr. Warren moves from white oxen (then repeats oxen before repeating white) to white road to white dust, and then from the white dust to dust stirred. The words help not only in presenting a concrete image—which is important in seeing the land—but in *feeling* the movement of the scene through repetition.

Repetition can occur as the same word, phrase, or even sentence. It can be contextual, like repeating something that happened in a different point of view or as a summary, as well. Repetition can be used to make a certain statement clear, or to emphasize its significance.

In fact, repetition, although looked down upon these days, is a legitimate literary device, so much so that there we are given different words for types of repetition: we have *anadiplosis*, which is repetition of the last word in a line or clause; *anaphora* is the repetition of words at the start of clauses; *diacope* is the repetition of words broken by some other words; *epimone* is the repetition of a phrase (typically a question) to stress a point; and there are more. Again, we suggest all prose writers also write and study poetry, where these forms of repetition can be practiced and honed.

So, what about repetition of phrasing, even when using a variety of different words, but when the phrasing itself is repetitive?

Here's such a passage from *A Voice from the River* by Dan Gerber:

> Russell remembered how he and Nick had passed like ghosts in the house, how Nick, coming home from a date, would sneak through the kitchen to avoid passing Russell's desk where he might be talking letters into the Dictaphone, how he'd hear Nick in the hall but wouldn't call to him, how he'd think to ask Nick about school but couldn't remember what subjects he was taking.

Here, we see Gerber repeating his entry into a statement: "…how Nick would sneak…" "…how he'd hear, but wouldn't…" "…how he'd think, but couldn't…" These repetitions drive home the idea that Russell and Nick "passed like ghosts in the house" without actually saying that over and over again. It's interesting to see how a particular author uses repetition one way, while another author might use repetition in another way. There are endless options!

Just because fiction isn't written in verse, like many poems, doesn't mean that your fiction writing shouldn't have rhythm. The more fiction authors are engaged in the sound, as well as the meaning, of their stories, the better their stories will turn out.

Rule 7: Avoid Writing Long, Complex Sentences

No comment.

We could go on and on and on and on about this rule and will a little later but, for right now, let's just get started!

We've talked about confusing the reader on several occasions so it shouldn't come as a surprise when we say that confusion is the major factor for this rule—one set out to restrict the length and complexity of your sentences. Confusing the reader is a big deal after all, and we want to avoid doing so. Once a reader—even your most loyal and patient one—can't follow what's happening in your novel, she will stop reading.

Another argument against using long or complex sentences is that they may slow the pacing of your novel. Writing long, complex sentences affects how a reader reads. This subject of long sentences has become a hot topic because the reading public has a tendency to become bored easily, especially in these speed-of-light days when everything is digital. Many, if not all, readers want a novel that moves along without dragging its feet. With the rise in popularity of the thriller novel, we see these trends proving themselves. Thrillers are all about action, sudden bursts of suspense and drama.

So, what can we do? How do we break this rule and not only get away with it, but *improve* a reader's reading experience in the process?

Well, not all long or complex sentences are confusing. Period. And not all of them slow the pace of the content.

Believe it or not, readers are more intelligent and more sophisticated than they have ever been. They *can* handle a complex sentence, even several of them in a row. In fact, we often see writers over compensating and keeping all their sentences short and easily digestible. But underestimating your reader, other than making you look as though you're talking down to them, will most likely make your writing choppy. And choppy writing can slow the pace even more than an ill-placed long sentence. So, as with other rules, it's more about balancing the long with the short sentences, rather than using all of one or all of the other.

Another element to consider with regard to this rule is your narrator or your viewpoint characters. What do they talk like? How do they speak? Do they use long drawn out sentences to express themselves or do they talk sparingly? We've all met people who actually speak in long sentences and we have no problem understanding them. Take a professor or scientist, for example. Will they always talk using short, simple sentences? Of course not.

And what about a narrative that is meant to be soothing? What if your intent is to slow the pace of your novel so that when you speed it back up again your reader gets ramped up right along with the action your characters are experiencing. Or what if you want to lull your reader into a false sense of security, only to then surprise them with a burst of quick sentences? An especially long, complex sentence can manipulate flow and pacing in a narrative unlike any other writing tool. But, let's not make this sound as though long or complex sentences actually do slow the work down every time. They do not.

Here's one of our favorite long, complex sentences from Philip Roth's *Goodbye Columbus*:

> So that Mr. Scapello would not descend upon the boy with his chalky fingers, I walked up the three flights to Stack Three, past the receiving room where rheumy-eyed Jimmy Boylen, our fifty-one-year-old boy, unloaded books from a cart; past the reading room, where bums off Mulberry Street slept over Popular Mechanics; past the smoking corridor where damp-

> browed summer students from the law school relaxed,
> some smoking, others trying to rub the colored dye
> from their tort texts off their fingertips; and finally,
> past the periodical room, where a few ancient ladies
> who'd been motored down from Upper Montclair now
> huddled in their chairs, pince-nezing over yellowed,
> fraying society pages in old old copies of the Newark
> News. Up on Stack Three I found the boy.

Look at how *physical* that complex sentence is. The physicality of the sentence is enough to make you run out of breath just after climbing the three flights of stairs. Mr. Roth keeps the reader moving with the character, right beside him, which keeps this movement employed in the writing. This passage does not slow the pace by any means. In fact, this is a fine example of a long, complex sentence actually speeding things up.

Also notice the short sentence at the end of the passage. After the long, searching journey, it's a way of bringing the reader back to the main storyline. Notice, too, how the sentence is reversed. Instead of writing "I found the boy up on Stack Three," Mr. Roth flips the sentence into a passive voice, keeping the reader's focus keenly on the boy (rather than where he found the boy).

Here's one more example, a long sentence from famed minimalist-writer Earnest Hemmingway. This is an excerpt from his book *The Sun Also Rises*:

> I wondered if there was anything else I might pray
> for, and I thought I would like to have some money,
> so I prayed that I would make a lot of money, and then
> I started to think how I would make it, and thinking
> of making money reminded me of the count, and I
> started wondering about where he was, and regretting
> I hadn't seen him since that night in Montmartre, and
> about something funny Brett told me about him, and
> as all the time I was kneeling with my forehead on
> the wood in front of me, and was thinking of myself
> as praying, I was a little ashamed, and regretted that
> I was such a rotten Catholic, but realized there was

nothing I could do about it, at least for a while, and maybe never, but that anyway it was a grand religion, and I only wished I felt religious and maybe I would the next time; and then I was out in the hot sun on the steps of the cathedral, and the forefingers and the thumb of my right hand were still damp, and I felt them dry in the sun.

We love this example. Hemingway is *known* for his sparse language and yet, he's not lost to the power of a good, long sentence. Here, he causes the reader to become fully involved with the character, his thoughts, his actions, his hopes, his prayers. Even though Hemingway's sentence uses abstract rather than the physical components as compared to Roth's sentence, Hemingway's still offers a sense of anxiety, of movement, as you work your way to the end.

When comparing these two examples, you might also notice that Roth used a handful of semicolons, where Hemingway used only one, toward the end. While not all long, complex sentences require a semicolon, it's important to consider their usage. Roth clearly used them to contain the various mini-experiences he encountered in his search for the boy. Hemingway, on the other hand, used his to give the reader a much-needed breath as well as a scene change, without removing the reader completely from the character's inner dialogue when he steps out of the cathedral.

Still not convinced Hemingway was a fan of the long sentence? Here's another one, also from *The Sun Also Rises*, describing a seasoned bullfighter in the decline of his career:

> Sometimes he turned to smile that toothed, long-jawed, lipless smile when he was called something particularly insulting, and always the pain that any movement produced grew stronger and stronger, until finally his yellow face was parchment color, and after his second bull was dead and the throwing of bread and cushions was over, after he had saluted the President with the same wolf-jawed smile and contemptuous eyes, and he handed his sword over the barrera to be wiped, and put back in its case, he passed through into

the callejon and leaned on the barrera below us, his head on his arms, not seeing, not hearing anything, only going through his own pain.

If you start to look for long sentences in contemporary fiction, you'll see them all over the place. From the most action-packed science fiction novel to the highest level of literature. Although editors might tell you to limit the number of long, complex sentences in your next novel, using such sentences wisely adds depth to your work that you won't achieve any other way.

Rule 8: Eliminate Dialect From Dialogue

"Heck, Maisy. Willn't we should? Willn't we wanna?"

Using dialect in a novel or story can be a tricky endeavor. Even though good dialogue should sound real, using dialect means the author is employing unusual spellings of words to get the reader to read phonetically. So, the words, as typed, aren't familiar looking, they don't bring up any particular image right away, and they don't come with an explanation. That's why this practice is looked down on. And, the more speech patterns are homogenized by television and radio, the less tolerant editors (and readers) appear to be to dialect.

Similar to the aversion toward dialect in dialogue is the use of foreign words in the writing of English-written novels. Often, when a writer uses a foreign word or phrase, they will either repeat the word or phrase in English, or they'll assume the reader will get the gist of the word or phrase based on how it's used in the sentence. Seldom will a reader have to look the word up. Context helps understanding.

However with dialect, none of the possibilities mentioned occur, so how would a reader know if what they're reading is a typo or that they have to *listen* to the word phonetically?

Stopping to understand what a word means or what an author is trying to say pulls the reader out of the story and makes them then focus on the text. It may even have set them off on a search trying to look up the word, which would be frustrating because they might not find it.

In the past, when most Americans were still familiar with the dialects being used, it was easy for an author to assume that the reader might follow along. But in today's world, that's not the case.

This is why this rule has gained popularity. If an editor stops reading for any reason, including trying to understand a word, the manuscript is threatened by rejection. So to avoid any and all possibility that someone might stop reading your work, the no dialect rule was created.

We think the no dialect rule is a fairly good rule with solid reasoning behind it. After all, there are other ways an author can illustrate the language of someone who doesn't speak English very well, or who pronounces words in a funny way. An author can alter sentence structure, use apostrophe slang like *ain't* or *nothing'*, and use improper English, such as *gonna* (as in, *going to*) or *lemme* (as in, *let me*). All of these tricks help us get over the hurdle of not using true dialect.

But this book is about how to break the rules. So let's do just that!

Our first suggestion to sidestep the possible problems that dialect might cause is for the author to choose fewer words to write in dialect than, say, Mark Twain did in his novel *The Adventures of Tom Sawyer*. Here's a typical passage in Mr. Twain's book:

> Oh I dasn't, Mars Tom. Ole missis she'd take an' tar
> de head off'n me. 'Deed she would.

Although readable and understandable, this passage slows the reader down considerably. The language is phonetically accurate but it pauses our eyes over each word in order to get used to the dialect. It's difficult to read without paying very close attention. If read aloud, the dialect sounds pretty authentic, but today's reader will find this too cumbersome and would not likely read it out loud in order to *hear* it.

Here's another example of a passage rife with dialect from D. H. Lawrence's *Sons and Lovers*:

> I've bin 'elpin' Anthony, an' what's think he's gen
> me? Nowt b'r a lousy hae'f-crown, an' that's ivry
> penny—

This sentence is even more difficult to read than Mark Train's sentence. It appears that Lawrence is trying to use a British accent as well as dialect. If that's true, Lawrence is compounding the issue. However, nonetheless, again, this shows how difficult writing in dialect can be for the reader.

Terry Persun's novel, *Sweet Song*, used dialect only as a tool to indicate the relative ignorance of a particular speaker. He knew of the pitfalls, but wanted to make his dialogue sound—even in the mind of the reader—as authentic as possible. Here's an example from that novel:

> But Bess, she hole tight, turnin' in circles until the all of us come down on Big Leon, stoppin' him. When we let 'im up off the floor he leave the shack for two days. 'Course he daren't leave the farm...

Notice the combination of the use of phonetic spellings (used only twice: *hole* instead of *hold*, and *daren't* for *dare not*) and chopping through the use of an apostrophe (*turnin'*, *stoppin'*, *'im*, and *'Course* instead of *Of course*). Terry sidesteps using *only* phonetic dialect (for example, he still used the word *until* rather than *'til*, which might have been more likely for the character to say) by also employing some of our dialect-avoidance suggestions above, like altering sentence structure. This balance creates and *atmosphere* of dialect, without spelling it all out. The reader then gets the gist of altered speech, but isn't so bogged down with phonetic spelling. The result is a passage less difficult to read than the other two.

What we suggest you do to break this rule is to be cautious about *how much* dialect you use. By choosing fewer words to write phonetically, the reader can get the feel for the dialect without it permeating every word.

We also suggest that you use other tools to employ the same effect on the reader. For example, describe the socio-economic status of a character through the use of their grammar. For instance, word combinations like *got no* or *ain't done* create a particular image in the reader's mind. Also, truncating words like *helping* to *helpin'* and *smelling* to *smellin'* can be used to similar effect.

Likewise, if you're writing a period piece, slang can help with the sound of a character. Words and combinations like *rad*, *groovy*, *boss*, *bunk*, *neato*, *egad*, *alas*, *awesome*, and *totally man*, all have their eras of use and can add flavor to your dialogue.

Regional phrases can be used the same way as slang. Where some people refer to their front porch, others refer to it as a stoop. People from Pennsylvania call their own state PA, but outsiders wouldn't know that. Different regions and how they refer to non-alcoholic drinks can show dialect as well. East coast people use the word *soda*, others say *soft drink*, people from the southwest use the word *pop*.

Overall, there are many ways to help your dialogue sound authentic even by using a dialectical word here and there without creating difficulty for the reader. Our takeaway for this rule is, if you're looking to use dialect, use it sparsely and consistently, while also employing other techniques such as sentence structure and slang to enhance the overall speech pattern of a character. A little can go a long way.

Rule 9: Don't Vary Your Dialogue Tags

"What'd you say," he laughingly said with false enthusiasm.

Dialogue tags are a very big issue these days with publishing professionals. As usual, editors probably make more fuss about them than they need to. Still, we need to remember this as a reason to either use dialogue tags or not.

So, what is the premise behind not varying your dialogue tags? The general consensus is this: the phrase *Jimmy said* is sufficient to let the reader know who is talking. *Said* is practically invisible. This premise goes on to mean that any word other than *said* is not invisible and, therefore, gets in the way of the action. Further, the premise assumes that if the scene is written well enough, we don't need any dialogue tag. If the scene and what Jimmy is saying reveals that Jimmy is sad, we don't need to write *Jimmy said sadly* or *Jimmy sobbed* at the end of his dialogue (this relates to our comments on adverbs in Chapter 3 and showing versus telling in Chapter 2).

Also, varying your dialogue tags can have your reader following the wrong action in your novel. For example, if your character is pointing a gun at the culprit and the culprit asks a question that uses a dialogue tag, such as the word *acknowledged* you might inadvertently take the reader out of the main action which is the pointing the gun. Let's play this idea out:

> The detective removed his gun when he saw Jake enter the room.
>
> "I've got you now," he said.
>
> Jake shook his head, "What is it that you think I've done?"
>
> The detective's arm pushed the gun closer toward Jake. "You killed my family," he acknowledged.

In this example, we show that any dialogue tag other than *said* slows the action down and pulls the reader back and forth between narration through dialogue tags and the dialogue itself.

In fact, the word *acknowledged* sounds as though the two characters may know each other, that they may be friends or business associates and possibly met on the street or somewhere.

Even if you wrote, *he answered*, the scene breaks down.

Now, how do you break this rule without causing action to slow down or to deter the reader's interest from that action?

If there is no lead-in to a situation, then a dialogue tag is helpful for the reader to know what's going on. Let's say your character walks into an office building and steps up to the receptionist and asks to see someone in sales. So far, the reader knows nothing about the receptionist, so when we use the dialogue tag *she barked* we get an idea of what type of person the receptionist is. If we only wrote *she said* then how would we feel if the main character responded poorly? We'd think the main character was a jerk. But, when the receptionist barks at our main character, we understand why she would be cold or rude in return.

Sometimes a dialogue tag provides important information on how a person is responding. In *The Martian* by Andy Weir there is a short conversation where a few scientists are trying to figure out what the main character is going to do:

> "...We'll see what he does tomorrow. Maybe he'll go back to the Hab."
>
> "Maybe," Mindy said unconvinced.

The word *unconvinced* is necessary to let the reader know how Mindy really feels.

In Stephen King's novel *Joyland*, King sometimes uses a dialogue tag other than said or asked. *"Bullshit!" Tom cried* is an example. Almost every book out there the author has used a dialogue tag at one time or another, but not *all* of the time.

It's easy to imagine how a passage would sound if the author used dialogue tags all the time. For instance, this next scene overuses dialogue tags and ends up jerking the reader all around.

> "Why are you here now?" she cried out.
> "I came to pick you up for our date," he laughed.
> "Well, I'm not quite ready," she hissed.
> "Should I come back?" he sighed.
> "In fifteen minutes," she exclaimed.

That type of dialogue gets pretty boring or even comical pretty quickly. We suggest you use those dialogue tags, but use them when you need them and when it is crucially important to relay something meaningful about the character or something foreshadowing.

Let's look at that first scene with the detective and the gun again but only include tags that evoke a sense of character or setting and that make the scene rather than breaking it.

> The detective pulled his gun when he saw Jake
> enter the room, "I've got you now."
> Jake sneered, "What do you think I've done?"
> The detective's hand shook but he pushed the
> gun closer toward Jake, "You killed my family."

We've tightened not only the dialogue, but the action tags that were originally placed before each instance of dialogue. Using action, rather than a plain dialogue tag, helps move the story forward while also conveying who is talking and what emotion is behind the dialogue. Of course, there may be times when using *said* or *asked* gets repetitive and starts to pull the reader out of the text. You might find this occurring when your sentences are short.

Notice the overuse of *said* in the following passage, which we believe makes for boring dialogue and dialogue tags.

"Not interested," he said.
"You sure?" I said.
"I couldn't do it," he said.
"One last time," I said.
"Never," he said.
"I could force you," I said.
"Try," he said.

You can see how these short sentences might be better served with other tags, fewer tags or none at all!

Equally, sometimes it's appropriate to switch a sentence around so that what you might use a dialogue tag as part of the description or action of the character. For example, instead of saying *"That's ridiculous," Bob laughed.* Why not say *Bob laughed. "That's ridiculous."* Or you can enhance this by saying *Bob looked at how Jim had presented the data and laughed. "That's ridiculous."*

All in all, when you use a dialogue tag that is other than *said* or *asked*, use them thoughtfully. And, rather than use a tag at all, try to present the character in action so that the reader already has their attention on the character when she speaks.

Rule 10: Shun The Exclamation Point
This is a ludicrous rule!!!

There's an idea out there that if you write well enough you don't have to use exclamation points. That your writing will lead the reader into a position where the reader knows that what you have written is an exclamation.

As you may have already guessed, this rule, like the others, has been developed so that writers won't abuse the issue. After all, one exclamation point after another would bore the reader. Doing so would be the written equivalent of crying wolf. Used too often, the intent of the exclamation point will lose its meaning and no one will be surprised by the punctuation. But thinking that you should never use an exclamation point creates hyper vigilance in recognizing when you *should* use one. When this happens, it might be prudent to reread your written work to see if an exclamation point *is* warranted.

As with any rule, we've read books where there are many exclamation points, as well as book that probably could have used a few more. Examples abound, so let's jump in and look at how a few authors have done away with this rule and have pulled it off.

Along with dialogue, an exclamation point adds that extra bit of *oomph* to a sentence. Here's a sentence from the science fiction novel *New Earth* by Ben Bova:

> "It actually uses the incoming radiation to power itself!"

Bova's sentence incorporates both italics, to emphasize the word 'uses' and an exclamation point. This might be to emphasize the way the character speaks (or yells) his words.

We believe part of the reason for the exclamation point is because of the conversation itself. Two scientists are discussing electromagnetic energy. Since both understand the dynamics of the subject matter, the only way to show excitement is in how one of the scientists responds. The exclamation point tells us that the particular scientist is adamant about what he's saying (and it also sidesteps the need for a clunky dialogue tag).

Here's another short sentence from *Something From the Nightside* by Simon R. Green:

> "Interfering little turd, meddling in the affairs of your betters!"

The use of Green's exclamation point might have been find used as a question or even as narrative.

However, by saying *"Interfering little turd,"* the author has already lead the reader into this interesting passage because we know the dialogue is coming from someone who is angry.

An important point to note is that the Green's book was accepted and published whether it had the exclamation point in it or not. So, even if your exclamation point reiterates the inferred action of the sentence, it can still be okay. Just use your exclamation points sparingly.

Simon R. Green uses a lot of exclamation points in his novel. Another example is this one:

> "They scare me. I can't...I can't move. I can't breath. I can't think!"

The character is so scared that he can't move or breath, but what's important is that he can't think—that's why the exclamation point is there. Breathing or moving can be overlooked, but not thinking is unbearable. He also ramps up to the exclamation point in steps rather than writing: I can't move! I can't breath! I can't think! Doing so emphasizes the final point of action in this dialogue.

Exclamation points are to be used intentionally, such as in these instances: when you don't want the reader to miss the point being made, when you want the reader to feel the jolt of the sentence when it reaches the end, or when the author feels that she needs to drive home the situation or the conversation. As with any of the rules you break, make sure you have a good reason and the reader will most likely go along with your decision to break the rule.

The takeaway? Think of an exclamation point as a streamlined way of using a dialogue tag—most often, the context of the story will provide the reader with what they need in order to understand the intensity or excitement of a scene. An exclamation point is used when context or a dialogue tag just won't serve the scene the way you need it to. So, every once in a while, you'll want to add some punch to the story and nothing will provide that punch quite like an exclamation point.

Before we leave this chapter, we want to touch briefly on something used in Ben Bova's book mentioned above—Bova's use of italics.

Often, italics are used to indicate a direct thought of a particular point of view character. Italics are also used for emphasis. In a way the italics act like an exclamation point. And, just like exclamation points, italics should be used with consciousness. Notice when you plan to use italics to emphasize a word. Reconsider whether or not the passage offers a way for the reader to emphasize a word or thought on her own. Ask, is the storyline good enough for the reader to get the point of the emphasis? Did the author truly need to point that one word out?

Remember, while writing your novel or story, anything that pulls the reader away from the page has the potential to stop the reader from reading further. Be very careful about what words you emphasize, what exclamation points you use, and how you approach your reader. In the case of exclamation points and italics, less is more.

Rule 11: Don't Head Jump

My name is Max Headroom-me, me, me!

Any good editor will tell you not to head jump, but what does that mean? Head-jumping means to change point of view within the same chapter, or paragraph, or even sentence. This rule is fairly new because older novels, the classics were often written in omniscient point of view (or the God's-eye point of view), which allows for the shifting from one character's point of view to another's without any warning (such as with a chapter or scene break).

And the reading public of that time may have been used to that type of writing, but today's audience finds point of view switching a challenge to follow and sometimes downright confusing. Today's audience would rather track one character's actions or thoughts at a time. This is why the rule is in place.

This rule is especially important today since any author can simply publish a novels by uploading the manuscript to an online platform (Kindle, Nook, iBook) with little to no editing beforehand. Authors who are not versed in how different points of view work and why, won't know how to use them correctly. But ignorance is not a good reason to break this rule. It's lazy to not study the craft in which you're trying to work. It's like building a car without an engine because you didn't know you needed one. Who would buy it? No one.

Like many rules explained in this book, the real point is to make it easy for the reader to get into the plot of the book or on board with the character, and then stay engaged all the way to the end of the book. Anything—a phrase, word, dialogue tag, punctuation, or error that jolts the reading from your story can cause them to stop reading. You don't want that to happen.

But as with the other rules, this one is easily broken and broken often. Writers must pay close attention to point of view so that they don't break the rule—not unless they want to, that is.

Writers can get around this rule with two basic techniques:

1. An author can alternate points of view between characters with an extra space between sections (or a symbol, like an asterisk), which alerts the reader that something is going to change. For instance, a point of view character shift, a scene shift, a location shift, or a time shift.

2. An author can alternate chapters between different points of view characters by labeling each chapter such as: Judy's Chapter, Bob's Chapter, The Winter of 1934, Mars—Earth date: March 15, 3537, Georgia on a Tobacco Plantation). You can use this method even for first person point of view novels.

Perhaps there has been a tragedy and the author chooses four characters in different locations to present their side of the story, with each chapter labeled with the location it covers. Or, it could be several children brought up in the same household and how differently they experienced their upbringing, with a child's name marking his or her chapters. Or, perhaps it's a time-travel story with characters in different time periods, with the chapters labeled with different dates in time. The options are endless.

Even when this method is used, it's often advised that an author not shift points of view within the same paragraph or sentence, or the reader may be bounced around so much that they become frustrated or confused and put the book down. But just like any rule, this one *has* been broken successfully.

We're going to jump right to some examples that break this rule. In *Snow Angels* by Stewart O'Nan, the author's paragraph alternates point of view within a sentence. Here goes:

> The burgers are hot and just as good as the real
> Burger Hut. Hers is medium, the outside charred,

just how she likes it; he's remembered that she loves onions and hates tomato. Eating, she notices that he's looking around like she is, checking everyone out as if they're spies.

In this passage, we are first given the omniscient narrator who says, *The burgers are hot and just as good as the real Burger Hut.* The next sentence starts in her point of view (*just how she likes it*), then goes into his head after the semicolon. (*he's remembered that she loves onions and hates tomato*). And then we go back into her point of view: *Eating, she notices...* Now, we see how the author has shifted from his internal thinking to hers. That's what we call head-jumping—shifting a sentence as though from one character's point of view to another's. This sentence can also be read as though it's all in her point of view, and that she's merely noticing that he has remembered that she loves onions. Note though, that a reader could easily get confused. In fact, it's our belief that O'Nan *wants* the reader to feel uncomfortable, maybe even a bit confused as to what's going on in this scene, just as he appears to do through many of his scenes. The characters in this novel are often confused. He's done this intentionally. Their relationships— many of them in this novel—are strained and uncomfortable.

O'Nan's writing style actually adds to the anxiety of the characters in *Snow Angels*, and it works very well, but what if you're reading a romance where the characters are supposed to be falling in love? Or any other novel, for that matter? Here is a section we've written in order to illustrate how confusing head-jumping can be:

Craig held Sharon tightly, wondering why he was even involved with her. Sharon thought he was the kindest man, and lay her head on his shoulder. She knew she was falling in love. He hardly liked her, but wanted to be nice. She thought that his hug meant that they'd be together forever, yet he just didn't want to let go because he didn't want to be rude. How long should he continue to hug her? Until she pulled away? His thoughts wandered, while hers were fixed on her growing love for him.

We hope most emerging writers can see how confusing the head-jumping might become in a very short while. And maybe this example is a bit extreme, but readers can become easily confused even when point of view shifts from paragraph to paragraph let alone within a single sentence.

If you've ever been reading dialogue and forgot who was speaking and had to go back to figure it out, *that's* the sort of interruption you will avoid by maintaining a singular point of view.

Again, though, knowing how and when to break this rule, how to incorporate varying points of view will raise your writing to a higher degree. Here's how Alice Hoffman does it in *The Red Garden*.

> William Brady headed the first expedition. He decided that he needed a wife before he set into the wild, western parts of Massachusetts, a ready partner to help carry the weight of the journey. He met Hallie in Boston a month after her arrival, and before another month had passed they said I do and started out west. Hallie had been fending for herself ever since leaving England. William was the first man to ask her for her hand, and she quickly agreed. She didn't believe in romance, but she did have faith in her own future. He was forty, she was seventeen. He had already failed at everything he had tried; she hadn't yet begun to live. Hallie had the impression that the marriage was a mistake on their wedding night, spent at a raucous inn near Boston harbor.

In this passage, Alice shifts from talking about William Brady to talking about Hallie, then back to William and again back to Hallie—all in one paragraph. And she does it expertly and without confusion.

Aside from the clarity of this passage, why is this a useful technique for Hoffman to have used? First, it signals to the reader that we are to pay attention to *both* characters—their marriage and their journey together—equally. It also adds juxtaposition to their character development. Told side-by-side, the reader gets a glimpse into both opinions about the marriage in a short, concise passage. William wanted company; Hallie said yes because he was the first to ask. *He was forty, she was seventeen. He had already failed at everything he had tried; she hadn't yet begun to live.* By head-jumping in this way, Hoffman is saying to the reader: "Look at how different these characters are." The comparison ends up serving as a source of intrigue—what will happen when these two very different people are put in a trying situation that has them at odds? Hoffman is setting us up to expect tension later on.

Another way in which head-jumping might be of use is to use it for the sake of comedy. Perhaps a couple is going to have dinner: John thinks they agreed to meet at 6:00. Mary thinks they agreed to meet at 7:00. The reader knows that John and Mary aren't on the same page. In addition to wanting to read on to see what happens when John thinks Mary stood him up, when the moment of confrontation does arrive, the author has the opportunity to add comedy to the scene. The reader, having the inside scoop, in turn has a degree of comedic distance. So, rather than being tied up in John's emotions had we only been in his head, we think it's funny when Mary doesn't understand his reaction to her being *late*. Shakespeare's *Comedy of Errors* uses this same technique with the audience—where the viewer has the inside scoop and watches the characters' lives turn to chaos amidst the misunderstandings.

As with our other rules, the takeaway is to be mindful when you head-jump—and practice! Get a few trusted readers to read your work and if they don't mention that they got confused or asked why you shifted from one character to another, that they wanted to read more… then you nailed it!

Rule 12: Shy From Using Prologues

Where do we even begin? Authors have been using prologues for ages, and now they're looked down upon. Why? Well because, like anything else, they can be abused. Some authors use the prologue to explain the story so that they can jump right into the action with chapter one. They think that they can get you hooked that way. Well, it doesn't work. Authors need to think of prologues as first chapters in that they can't be boring. If a reader can't get through the prologue because it's just a litany of facts, then they won't even get to chapter one where the action begins. Or, they'll skip the prologue and go right to chapter one, then later on not understand certain nuances of the story because they didn't want to slog through the information-dump in the prologue. Either way, in this case, a prologue is hurting the book rather than helping it.

Prologues should not be used to provide a synopsis of the story, either—this is another reason editors tell authors not to include a prologue. If the story is strong, and if the author knows how to build the world they're writing about, then a prologue isn't needed. It becomes redundant. A good writer should be able to include world building, back-story, and anything else necessary to the novel without having to separate it out like a sidebar and put it into the front of the story. A prologue is not the book. It's often written in a telling, not showing, technique.

So these are ways a prologue fails, if you will. How it abuses its upfront placement in the novel. How it falls flat. So, how can it shine?

As we've said, prologues appear in a lot of novels, including contemporary stories. What makes them work? Here's the beginning of a prologue—not told, but shown—in a recent *Deathlands* saga, *Plague Lords* by James Axler (*Deathlands* novels are series novels with several actual authors—James Axler is the house name used on all the books, not the actual author.)

> When a mosquito speared Okie Moore right between the eyes, he deftly squashed it against his forehead. Blood from the bug's crushed abdomen trickled in a cool bead down the side of his nose. He wiped it across his cheek with the back of his hand, smearing a fresh daub of red into the impasto of squashed bodies, legs, wings—tiny gobs of black mush trapped in the hairs of his beard. A cloud of bugs wheeled around his head.

This passage could easily begin the novel as chapter one, so why is it a prologue? Because the main character doesn't show up in this passage (the main character arrives in chapter one). And because this prologue is meant to show a pending threat. The people in a prologue like this may never show up in the novel again—they're meant to reveal something about the story, something the reader could not learn through the main character or viewpoint character.

A common use of the prologue in novels today is to introduce a situation, event, technology, person, or place. An introduction isn't connected to the main plot of the novel except for one or two elements. In *Excavation* by James Rollins, he shows us an event that happened in the past.

> There was no escape.
>
> Crashing through the misty jungle, Francisco de Almagro had long given up all prayer of ever outrunning the hunters who dogged his trail. Panting, he crouched along the thin path and caught his breath. He wiped the sweat from his brow with his sleeve. He

still wore his Dominican robe, black wool and silk,
but it was stained and torn.

In this novel, the story from the past is integral to what happens to the characters in the present. The details are important, even though the character introduced is the prologue is long gone by the time we enter the main part of the story. Chapter one begins in the present, but the storyline eventually harkens back to that prologue to tie things together.

Prologues must have a purpose other than to shortcut writing the actual novel. That's why most novels don't have a prologue. But when one is necessary, no editor or publisher in their right mind would reject the book just for having one. The takeaway for this rule? Don't use a prologue for info-dumping—use it to enhance the story later on.

BONUS RULES

Rule 13: Avoid Clichés

If you've seen one cliché, you've seen 'em all!

All the rules we've discussed are good rules to consider while you're writing. But they are not rules you have to completely abide by. This rule, like the others, was put into place to keep your writing from becoming boring and unimaginative. Clichés are present for a reason. They're familiar. Everyone uses them. They represent a belief system as much as a saying. "You can't teach an old dogs new tricks" is a belief that once you've reached a certain age, it's not possible (or at least more difficult) to teach you anything new. It's metaphor for a lot of other things, too, depending on how you use it.

Clichés are used all the time, so why not use them in writing? Well, *because they are used all the time.* Using a cliché removes the need for creativity, and can make your writing sound as though you've put no time into it at all. Clichés are trite, commonplace, unimaginative. Used too often, a cliché sucks all the creativity out of your writing. And because they often have a wide array of meanings, they can also, sometimes, confuse your reader.

Here are a few clichés that writers are encouraged to delete from their work:
- avoid it like the plague
- dead as a doornail
- every dog has its day

- like a kid in a candy store
- think outside the box
- the pot calling the kettle black
- take the tiger by the tail
- as light as a feather

This begs the question, when is it okay to use a cliché? As with many of the rules discussed in this little book, a cliché should be used seldom...that is unless you are using them in the mouths of your characters. Let's say a first person character is a stereotype, and you wish to elaborate on the person's lack of originality by having him or her use clichés all of the time. The character's mindless banter can be annoying, which may be what you want. In this case, your book could be riddled with clichés and it would be okay.

Another reason you might use a cliché is if you're writing a spoof. Beginning a book with, "it was a dark and stormy night" would set the tone for the whole novel. Similarly, starting with, "once upon a time" would alert the reader that he or she is about to enter a fairytale world.

Using a cliché is all right as long as you know it's a cliché and you're being conscious about using it. For example, it might be used as a shortcut once or twice in a book. You could just as easily use a cliché to get a point across without belaboring the detail. Let's say someone in your story picks up a metal block that should weigh several pounds. Saying, "it's as light as a feather" might be the most appropriate response so that you can move your story forward without thinking twice. Although you could be more creative and come up with a way to say that the metal block was unusually light for it's size, that it's lightness surprised your character and she almost threw it into the air, you may not always want to.

Although there are always ways to avoid a cliché, it's not always necessary. Using a cliché can even make your characters sound like real people, since most of us use a cliché every once in a while. We've looked for clichés used in contemporary novels and have found very few but that doesn't mean you must avoid using them yourself. Be conscious of what you're writing, who's voice you're writing through, and you'll be fine.

Rule 14: Don't Use Onomatopoeia

Onomatopoeia are those words that, when pronounced, they sound like the sound they are suggesting. The *hum* of bees, the *pop* of a balloon, the *screech* of the chalk on the chalkboard. The use of onomatopoeia can reduce your text to the level of cliché, preempting the use of more creative images or expressions. Like other rules in this book, using onomatopoeia can become a lazy habit. Used too often, and your text will sound silly or mundane, at best.

Here is an example that would be awkward and odd to read:

> The recorder went bloop into the ocean a moment before he splashed in after it. His partner, stood in the drizzle, a continual drip, drip of moisture falling from his suit. The boat shifted and a spray of water drenched him.

Not terrible, perhaps, but way too many noises going on. And perhaps that's part of the problem. Although we want to include sound, too many sounds would just create noise.

So, when can you use onomatopoeia and not abuse the readers' sensibilities?

Infrequently comes to mind. Creating a scene is more than just images or sounds. Expanding your writing to include other senses helps to round out a scene. But, when you need a specific sound, something familiar that your reader will quickly understand, that's when onomatopoeia comes in handy. Here are a few that, in the right context, would work perfectly.

Say a criminal is trying to be discreet when he drops a body into the river. This might be a telling sentence: *The body made a splash when it hit the water.* Yikes, a splash is not quiet. This sentence might alert the reader that someone may have heard the splash. Another example could be that a man who is trying to fall asleep can't seem to get his mind to stop running or his ears from listening: "He heard the drip, drip of the downstairs' faucet." Again, this would be clear and the reader would be able to identify with the sentence. In these two cases, coming up with some fancy or creative way of delivering the information might be worse than using onomatopoeia.

We mentioned E. L. Doctorow's passage from *Homer and Langley* earlier in Chapter 2, and want to point out, again, those last few lines as Homer goes blind:

> ...and then all my sight was gone though I could hear clearly the scoot scut of the blades on the ice, a very satisfying sound, a soft sound though full of intention, a deeper tone than you'd expect made by the skate blades, perhaps for having sounded the resonant basso of the water under the ice, scoot scut, scoot scut.

Beautifully written, Doctorow's writing takes the reader from sight and image to only sound, as the main character becomes blind. The *scoot scut* sound becomes extremely relevant and important. This paragraph sets up the novel as a sound-focused book. There are all types of images presented, of course, but all along the way, we, the readers, can also hear the surroundings even when not explicitly written.

Rule 15: Shun Rhyme In Prose

This rule reads more like: restrict your use of rhyme in prose. The basic idea with this rule is not to use poetic devices in prose. This has nothing to do with what some readers call *poetic language*, but with actual alliteration, rhyme, repetition (which we mentioned in an earlier chapter), sibilance, assonance, consonance, etc. The use of these devices can jar the reader, for sure, and if not done well, can start to read as a spoof. Of course, there are a lot of poetic devices that do cross over into fiction without being questioned, such as simile, metaphor, and imagery. But when it comes to sound-based devices like rhyme and the others mentioned above, crossover from poetry to prose is not nearly so common.

Using rhyme in prose can force a cadence on the reader that the author doesn't want. Continually rhyming sentence after sentence or phrase after phrase removes a lot of the tension in the story, placing that tension, instead, on the proper use of rhyme. Rhyme also eliminates a lot of structure, especially when you're writing for the rhyme scheme and not plot or characterization. Anything over-done becomes noticeable, and therefore takes the readers out of the story being told. This is never a good thing.

Rhyme can be used to create humor. It can be used to accentuate the quirkiness of a character, and it can be used to draw the reader into the world of a maniac. Like every one of the rules in this book, rhyming should be used consciously. Have a reason you wish to use rhyme. As mentioned above, if your main character is on the verge of going completely insane, he or she might start speaking in nursery rhymes. This could be eerily appropriate, making the reader uneasy every time it happens. A scene calling for comic relief might invite a funny rhyme, too.

And there is one other place we haven't mentioned that we must. It's where rhymed prose is almost a requirement sometimes: children's picture books. "I do not like green eggs and ham! I do not like them, Sam-I-am."

Rule 16: Evade Using Flashbacks

Our understanding of this rule is that editors and readers don't want to have a chapter long, or multi-chapter flashback in the middle of your novel. This is partly due to how distracting it is to the reader. It's true that most readers enjoy a chronologically sound novel so that they don't have to reconstruct their concept of the main character halfway through the book. And, as many of these rules advise, using too many flashbacks can be downright confusing.

If a particular event from childhood had an impact on your character, it's often fairly easy to include a few quick lines to explain it. Like this:

> The rejection reminded him of his first love in third grade and how Jamie not only refused to hold his hand, but yelled how icky he was to the whole classroom. He was humiliated, and had never forgotten how that felt.

It's not necessary to recreate the entire scene, including the schoolroom, the situation, the other children standing around. There's no need to provide information about how he got to school, or his interactions with his family. If the situation can be distilled down to a few sentences, then why not do that?

Flashbacks that are longer than a few sentences are rare. Books that *do* handle long flashbacks well are those where multiple situations piled one atop another add up to a really traumatic situation for the character. In this case, the flashback could cover a few chapters to drive home why the character is a serial killer, a policeman, someone who has gone insane, etc. In this case, a few short sentences may not be enough to get across the depth of the events that took place. After all, a sentence like—*That year she was beaten almost to death in an alley, expelled from college for smoking pot, lost her father and her mother to cancer, and found that her boyfriend had been cheating on her with her best friend*—might be too much information in too short a space. It might be so much information, in fact, that the reader doesn't actually *feel* any of it the way the author would like. Drawing each of the events out in longer flashbacks would most likely be the best way to go. This would give the book a timeless feel to it, but that could be an advantage, too.

Rule 17: Don't Include Too Much Sex, Swearing, Drug Use, Violence, Contemplation, Etc.

The *way too much* syndrome. If you've ever read an adult sex book, you probably have an idea of what this rule is all about. Too much of any one thing can make the whole novel read the same—where nothing new happens. It doesn't matter whether we're talking about everyone using drugs or everyone having sex, gone too far the text all starts sounding the same, and there's no arc, no forward motion, nothing. At a certain point, the shock (or other intended effect) of the act loses its power.

It seems to us that this is pretty self-evident, yet we've heard editors complain about it. In fact, we've heard readers complain that a novel is "like reading one action scene after another until they all run together and you don't care about anyone." Yeah, you've read those books. Some books are so focused on the idea that the people all sit around and discuss the idea instead of moving about, interacting with the outside world, or actually *doing* something. Such books are more like textbooks than novels. And then, like mentioned above, there are the adult sex novels where there is little plot, only enough to hold together one explicit sex scene after another. Each chapter is pretty much the same as the chapter before it.

We've mentioned the too fast, too slow, too-much-sex, too-much-talk books above as though they don't work, but sometimes they do. And that's when the rule is broken. Let's face it, there are readers who enjoy every one of the types of books we've mentioned. The readership might be small, but it's there. The idea is how to do it differently than other books on the market. Or to create such unique characters or character voices that a reader will stick with it. So, perhaps too much action isn't an issue if the main character is interesting enough to carry the novel forward in a unique way. Perhaps slow and plodding dialogue can be overlooked if the idea is so fantastic or engaging that the reader can't wait to find out more. And perhaps all that swearing is necessary because the story would be unrealistic without it.

Writing skills are important in every one of the rules we've mentioned in this book, and there is no escaping the need to learn the craft of writing so that you can break the rules without it ever being noticed.

Final Thoughts

Tom Robbins once said that "storytelling is not writing." What we think he's alluding to are all the rules we've talked about so far. If storytelling was all any of this was about, it wouldn't matter if you used too many clichés, if you included flashbacks larger than the original story. But writing is more than storytelling. And this is how we'd like to end up with this book: with the understanding that storytelling isn't bad, it's often necessary in your novel, but it isn't writing, it isn't craft. Writing is a skill that includes both sides of your brain, the analytical or language side, as well as the creative and imaginative side. The two must work together to write.

We like to think of writing as a skill, a craft, and a talent. Just because you know the techniques and methods needed to have some skill in writing, doesn't mean that you are good at the craft, which takes a deeper understanding to fine tune the writing. And just because you can fine-tune your writing doesn't mean you have the talent to take that work to the next level in terms of story.

That's what we've been discussing here: taking your writing to the next level. You probably already have the basic skills to form a sentence and to line them up so that they tell some type of story. You may even have enough craft knowledge where you can pull out just the right tools to use while writing. Talent is when you pull everything together to produce something no one else could produce. It takes knowing all the rules, why they're there, and how to break them. It takes practice breaking the rules to fully understand how to break them well.

In all our combined lives, we've been constant students of writing. And there is no end in site. There is always more to learn. Our suggestion is that you read books on how to write, that you take classes on how to write, go to conferences, to college, to talks. Stay current by reading and reading and reading. After all, you're a writer, and when you're working on your next novel, it's critical that you know what else is out there and how you're going to make it better.

Now, go break some rules.

END

ABOUT THE AUTHORS

Nicole J. Persun started her professional writing career at the age of sixteen with her young adult novel, A Kingdom's Possession, which later became an Amazon Bestseller. Her second novel, Dead of Knight, won Gold in Foreword Magazine's 2013 Book of the Year Award. Aside from novels, Nicole has had short stories, flash fiction, poetry, and essays published in a handful of literary journals. She often speaks at libraries, writer's groups, and writer's conferences across the country. Currently working on a Master's degree at the Northwest Institute of Literary Arts, Nicole lives in Washington State.

www.NicoleJPersun.com

#1 Amazon bestseller, **Susan Wingate**'s writing has been hailed by international bestselling author Michael Collins as "writing of the finest quality." Susan Wingate's work has appeared in many literary journals such as her ethereal poem *"The Dance of Wind in Trees"* which appeared in the April 2013 issue of the *Virginia Quarterly Review*. Susan's popular and award-winning stories include *Bobby's Diner*, *Drowning*, and her latest novel, *The Deer Effect* which won three book awards in 2015—the category of religious fiction in the eLit Book Award, the category of Christian fiction in the Pacific Book Award, and a finalist award for the category of inspirational fiction in the Next Generation Indie Book Award. You can find Susan on Facebook and Twitter.

www.SusanWingate.com

Terry Persun has studied engineering, conscious dreaming, shamanism, numerology, and many other subjects. He has a Bachelor's of Science degree and a Master's in Arts in Creative Writing. Besides writing nonfiction, Terry has been writing and publishing short stories and novels since the early 1970s. He has been the recipient of seven novel and poetry awards over the years, including the Star of Washington Award, a Silver IPPY for historical fiction, two Book of the Year Finalist Awards, two Finalist Awards from the USABookNews International Book Awards, two poetry chapbook awards, and a Jeanne Voge Poetry Award. Terry writes in a variety of genres, including science fiction, thriller, mystery, and mainstream fiction. He is a respected keynoter and speaker at libraries, writers' groups, writers' conferences, and universities across the country.

www.TerryPersun.com

Works by Nicole Persun
Fantasy:
Dead of Knight
A Kingdom's Posession

Works by Susan Wingate
Christian Fiction:
The Deer Effect

Family Drama/
Women's Fiction:
Drowning

Mystery:
Bobby's Diner
Hotter than Helen
Sacrifice at Sea

Noir Mystery:
Of the Law

Young Adult Fantasy:
Spider Brains

Works by Terry Persun
Mainstream Novels:
Wolf's Rite
Giver of Gifts
Deception Creek
The Witness Tree
The Perceived Darkness

Historical Novels:
Sweet Song
Ten Months in Wonderland

Science Fiction Novels:
Hear No Evil
Revision 7:DNA
Backyard Aliens
Cathedral of Dreams
The Killing Machine

Fantasy Novels:
Doublesight
Memory Tower
Fugitives
Gargoyle
The NSA Files
The Voodoo Case

Mystery/Detective Novels:
Mistake in Identity
Man by the Door

Short Story Collections:
Abstract Paintings

Poetry Collections:
Sentences
And Now This
Every Leaf
Barn Tarot
Problems with Opaque

Nonfiction:
Guidebook for Working with
Small Independent Publishers
Make Money Writing
Simple Practices for a More
Successful and Fulfilling Life
Divine Magnetics

www.ingramcontent.com/pod-product-compliance
Lightning Source LLC
Chambersburg PA
CBHW070437290526
45791CB00005B/2007